VOLUME **11**

PLAY 8 SONGS WITH A PROFESSIONAL BAND

D0504037

HOW TO USE THE CD:

Each song has <u>two</u> tracks:

1) Full Stereo Mix

All recorded instruments are present on this track.

2) Split Track

Piano and **Bass** parts can be removed
by turning down the volume on the LEFT channel.

Guitar and **Harmonica** parts can be removed
by turning down the volume on the RIGHT channel.

ISBN 978-1-4234-9471-3

7777 W. BLUEMOUND RD. P.O. BOX 13819 MILWAUKEE, WI 53213

Visit Hal Leonard Online at
www.halleonard.com

CHRISTMAS BLUES

BOOK

CD

Back Door Santa

Words and Music by Marcus Lewis Daniel
and Clarence George Carter

4

BUT ONCE A YEAR. BUT I'LL COME RUN-NIN' WITH MY PRES-ENTS
EV-'RY TIME YOU CALL ME DEAR. I KEEP SOME

BRIDGE

CHANGE IN MY POCK-ET IN CASE THE CHIL-DREN WERE AT HOME. I GIVE THEM A FEW PEN-NIES SO
WE CAN BE A-LONE. I LEAVE THE BACK DOOR O-PEN SO IF AN-Y-BOD-Y SMELLS A MOUSE WOULD-N'T OL'

CHORUS

SAN-TA BE IN TROU-BLE IF IT AIN'T NO CHIM-NEY IN THE HOUSE. I'M A BACK DOOR SAN-TA.
MAKE MY RUNS A-BOUT THE BREAK O' DAY.
I MAKE THE WOM-EN HAP-PY WHILE THE MEN ARE OUT AT PLAY.

GUITAR SOLO

To CODA   D.S. AL CODA   CODA

I KEEP SOME

5

Christmas Time

Words and Music by Bruce Iglauer,
Ed Williams and James Young

Additional Lyrics

2. Don't your ornaments look pretty
Hangin' on your Christmas tree?
I don't know 'bout no one else,
They sure look good to me.
Give me some of yours,
I'll give you some of mine,
'Cause it's Christmas time.

3. I got a big ol' candy cane
That you'd like to lick.
If you take your time,
Ooh, that'll do the trick.
Now give me some of yours,
I'll give you some of mine,
'Cause it's Christmas time.

Dig That Crazy Santa Claus

CD TRACK
- 4 Full Stereo Mix
- 12 Split Mix

C Version

Words and Music by Albert Johnston Jr.,
Leon Rene and Rafael Rene

Intro
Fast Shuffle ♩ = 188

1. Dig that cra-zy San-ta Claus, with his red suit on.
2., D.S. See additional lyrics

Dig that walk, that cra-zy talk. A man, oh, man, he's real-ly gone.

Chorus

Cool it, Ru-dolph, cool it, a with your nose a-glow.

Tell those groov-y rein-deer, when San-ta starts to blow, go, go.

Coda 1

Interlude

Christ-mas Eve. Jump.

VERSE

3. DIG THAT CRA - ZY SAN - TA CLAUS, _____ A WITH HIS RED SUIT
4., D.S.S. SEE ADDITIONAL LYRICS

ON. I DIG THAT WALK, A THAT A CRA - ZY TALK. _____

MAN, OH MAN, HE'S REAL - LY GONE. _____ I JUMP _ FOR JOY. _____ COOL _

CHORUS

_____ IT, RU - DOLPH, COOL _____ IT, _____ WITH YOUR NOSE A - GLOW. _____

TELL THOSE GROOV-Y REIN - DEER, WHEN SAN - TA STARTS TO BLOW. GO, GO. I

Coda 2

Outro

CHRIST - MAS EVE. _____

ADDITIONAL LYRICS

2., 4. DIG THAT CRAZY SANTA CLAUS WITH HIS BAG OF TOYS.
DRAGS HIS SACK THROUGH A CHIMNEY STACK,
ALL THE LITTLE HEP-CATS JUMP FOR JOY.

D.S., D.S.S. DIG THAT CRAZY SANTA CLAUS, WELL I DO BELIEVE
HE WILL BRING SOME CRAZY TOYS.
YOU BETTER BE GOOD THIS CHRISTMAS EVE.

Merry Christmas, Baby

Words and Music by Lou Baxter
and Johnny Moore

Please Come Home for Christmas

Words and Music by Charles Brown
and Gene Redd

VERSE
MODERATELY SLOW ♩. = 57

BELLS WILL BE RING-IN', THE GLAD, GLAD NEWS. OH WHAT A

CHRIST-MAS TO HAVE THE BLUES. MY BA-BY'S GONE.

I HAVE NO FRIENDS TO WISH ME GREET-

- INGS. OOH, ONCE A-GAIN. CHOIRS WILL BE SING-

CHORUS

IN'. SI - LENT NIGHT. CHRIST-MAS
ME, YOU'LL NEV - ER MORE ROAM? CHRIST-MAS AND

CAR - OLS BY CAN - DLE - LIGHT. PLEASE, COME HOME
NEW YEAR WILL FIND YOU HOME.

FOR CHRIST-MAS. PLEASE COME HOME FOR CHRIST-MAS. IF NOT FOR

Santa Baby

By Joan Javits,
Phil Springer and Tony Springer

CD TRACK
7 Full Stereo Mix
15 Split Mix

C Version

VERSE

3. San-ta ba-by, I want a yacht, and real-ly that's not a lot.
4., 5., 6. See additional lyrics

Been an an-gel all year, San-ta ba-by, so hur-ry down the chim-ney to-night.

To Coda | 1., 2. | 3.

BRIDGE

Come and trim my Christ-mas tree with some dec-o-ra-tions bought at

Tif-fa-ny's. I real-ly do be-lieve in you,

D.S. al Coda

Coda

OUTRO

Let's see if you be-lieve in me.

Hur-ry down the chim-ney to-night.

Hur-ry to-night.

Additional lyrics

2. Santa baby, a '54 convertible too, light blue,
I'll wait up for you, dear.
Santa baby, so hurry down the chimney tonight.

4. Santa honey, one little thing I really need: the deed
to a platinum mine.
Santa baby, so hurry down the chimney tonight.

5. Santa cutie, and fill my stocking with a duplex and checks,
sign your X on the line.
Santa cutie, and hurry down the chimney tonight.

6. Santa baby, forgot to mention one little thing, a ring.
I don't mean on the phone.
Santa baby, so hurry down the chimney tonight.

17

Outro

Additional Lyrics

2. Got my baby, my precious love,
Happiness, good God, I got plenty of.
Would you believe I got peace of mind?
And I'll be groovin' at Christmas time.
Merry Christmas, Happy New Year.

3. Hope you have a good cheer.
I love you, James Brown love you.
Your luck is so and so, missin' you.
Brother love, ow, ow.

4. Soulful Christmas, like a sweet melody,
I'm a lucky so and so, the bells gonna ring for me.
Merry Christmas and a Happy New Year
To all of my fans, have good cheer.
I love you, I love you, won't take nobody else.
I can't stand myself, huh, good God.

5. I got a heart full of love for the whole wide world,
And a little special love, a little soulful girl.
I got this feelin' every, every now and then
Gotta get ready, bring the New Year in.
Merry Christmas and a Happy New Year.

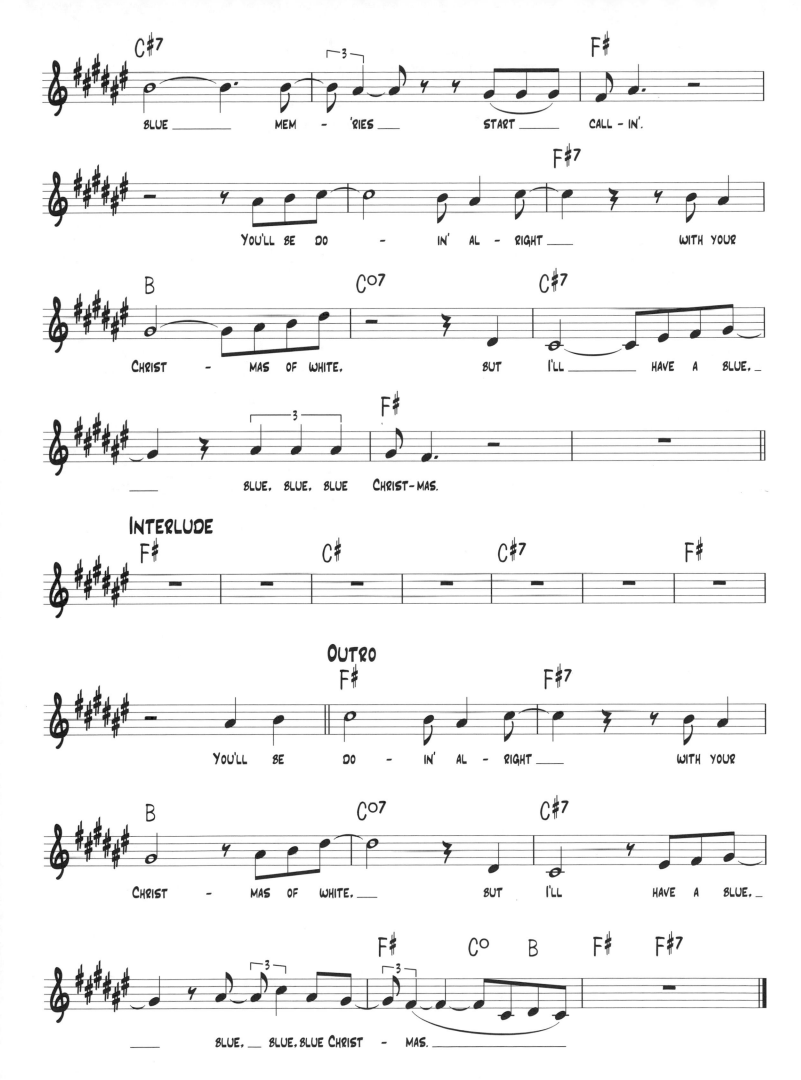

Christmas Time

Words and Music by Bruce Iglauer,
Ed Williams and James Young

ADDITIONAL LYRICS

2. DON'T YOUR ORNAMENTS LOOK PRETTY
HANGIN' ON YOUR CHRISTMAS TREE?
I DON'T KNOW 'BOUT NO ONE ELSE,
THEY SURE LOOK GOOD TO ME.
GIVE ME SOME OF YOURS,
I'LL GIVE YOU SOME OF MINE,
'CAUSE IT'S CHRISTMAS TIME.

3. I GOT A BIG OL' CANDY CANE
THAT YOU'D LIKE TO LICK.
IF YOU TAKE YOUR TIME,
OOH, THAT'LL DO THE TRICK.
NOW GIVE ME SOME OF YOURS,
I'LL GIVE YOU SOME OF MINE,
'CAUSE IT'S CHRISTMAS TIME.

26

Additional lyrics

2., 4. Dig that crazy Santa Claus with his bag of toys.
Drags his sack through a chimney stack,
All the little hep-cats jump for joy.

D.S., D.S.S. Dig that crazy Santa Claus, well I do believe
He will bring some crazy toys.
You better be good this Christmas Eve.

MERRY CHRISTMAS, BABY

CD TRACK

5 Full Stereo Mix
13 Split Mix

B♭ Version

Words and Music by Lou Baxter
and Johnny Moore

MY STER-E-O. ____ WELL, I WANT TO KISS YOU BA - BY,

WHILE YOU'RE STAND - IN' BE - NEATH ____ THE MIS-TLE-TOE.

SOLOS

VERSE

2. SAINT NICK CAME DOWN THE CHIM - NEY, A - BOUT A HALF PAST THREE, __

LEFT ALL THESE PRET-TY PRES-ENTS THAT YOU SEE BE-FORE ME. _____ OOH.

MER - RY CHRIST-MAS, BA - BY, SURE __ BEEN GOOD TO ME. _____

Outro

I HAVE-N'T HAD A DRINK THIS MORN-IN', I'M ALL LIT UP. __

I'M ALL LIT UP, __ OOH. _____ LIKE A CHRIST-MAS TREE.

CD TRACK

6 Full Stereo Mix

14 Split Mix

B♭ Version

Please Come Home for Christmas

Words and Music by Charles Brown and Gene Redd

Santa Baby

By Joan Javits,
Phil Springer and Tony Springer

VERSE

3. San-ta ba-by, I want a yacht, and real-ly that's not a lot.
4., 5., 6. See additional lyrics

Been an an-gel all year, San-ta ba-by, so hur-ry down the chim-ney to-night.

To Coda ⊕ | 1., 2. | 3.

BRIDGE

Come and trim my Christ-mas tree with some dec-o-ra-tions bought at Tif-fa-ny's. I real-ly do be-lieve in you.

D.S. al Coda

⊕ Coda

OUTRO

Let's see if you be-lieve in me. Hur-ry down the chim-ney to-night.

Hur-ry to-night. Hur-ry to-night.

Additional lyrics

2. Santa baby, a '54 convertible too, light blue.
I'll wait up for you, dear,
Santa baby, so hurry down the chimney tonight.

4. Santa honey, one little thing I really need: the deed
to a platinum mine.
Santa baby, so hurry down the chimney tonight.

5. Santa cutie, and fill my stocking with a duplex and checks.
Sign your X on the line.
Santa cutie, and hurry down the chimney tonight.

6. Santa baby, forgot to mention one little thing, a ring.
I don't mean on the phone.
Santa baby, so hurry down the chimney tonight.

Outro

F7

YEAR. ALL GOOD CHEER. THERE'S ONE MORE THING, YOU BEEN SO NICE

TO ME DOWN ___ THROUGH THE YEARS. ___ AND I'LL AL-WAYS RE-

MEM-BER YOU. ___ WELL I'LL NEV-ER FOR-GET, YOU BOUGHT MY REC-ORDS, COME TO SEE MY SHOW.

THAT'S ___ WHY JAMES ___ BROWN ___ LOVE YOU ___

___ SO. YOU COME TO SEE MY SHOW. ___ THAT'S A DEBT THAT I'LL AL - WAYS

OWE. ___ COME TO SEE MY SHOW. ___ SEE YOU AT CHRIST-MAS, COME TO SEE MY

SHOW. SEE MY SHOW. ___

Additional Lyrics

2. Got my baby, my precious love,
   Happiness, good God, I got plenty of.
   Would you believe I got peace of mind?
   And I'll be groovin' at Christmas time.
   Merry Christmas, Happy New Year.

3. Hope you have a good cheer.
   I love you, James Brown love you.
   Your luck is so and so, missin' you.
   Brother love, ow, ow.

4. Soulful Christmas, like a sweet melody,
   I'm a lucky so and so, the bells gonna ring for me.
   Merry Christmas and a Happy New Year
   To all of my fans, have good cheer.
   I love you, I love you, won't take nobody else.
   I can't stand myself, huh, good God.

5. I got a heart full of love for the whole wide world.
   And a little special love, a little soulful girl.
   I got this feelin' every, every now and then
   Gotta get ready, bring the New Year in.
   Merry Christmas and a Happy New Year.

Back Door Santa

Words and Music by Marcus Lewis Daniel and Clarence George Carter

Blue Christmas

Words and Music by Billy Hayes and Jay Johnson

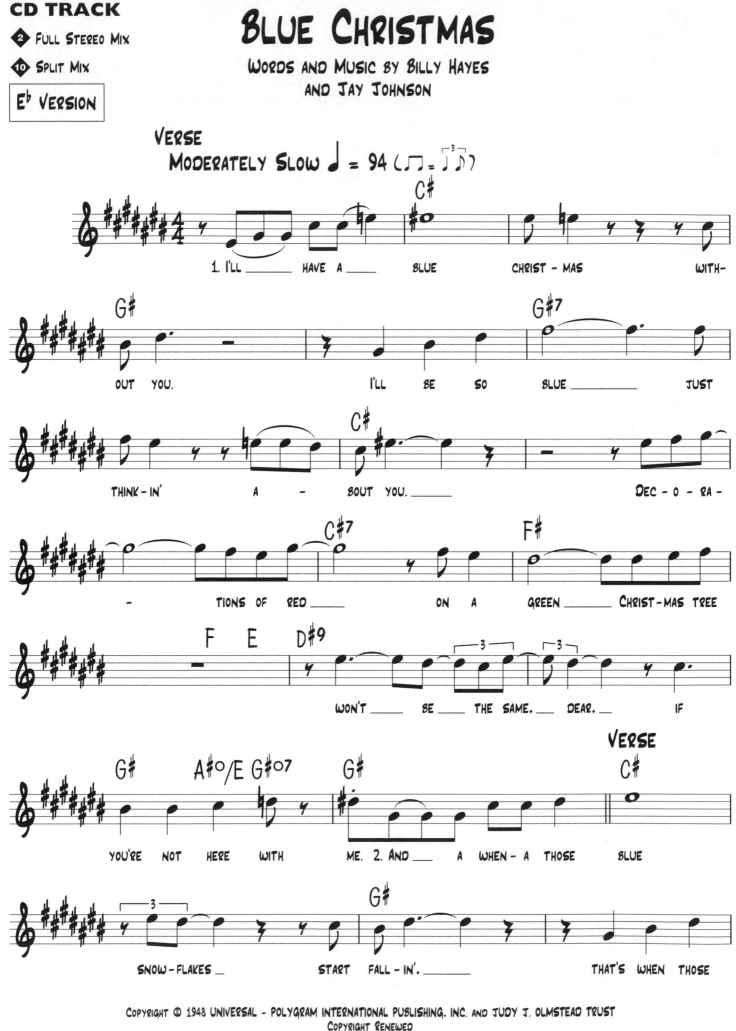

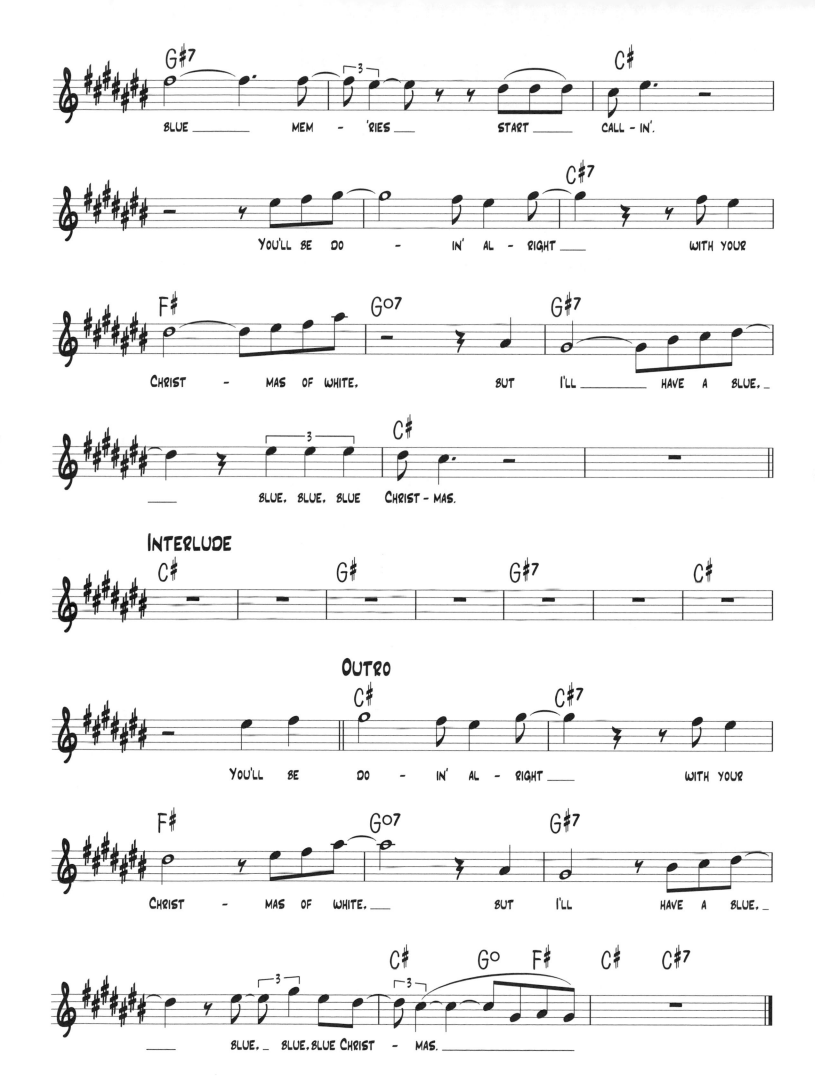

Christmas Time

Words and Music by Bruce Iglauer, Ed Williams and James Young

Guitar Solo

B7　E9　B7　F#9　F9

To Coda ⊕

E9　B7

4. Let me slide be-tween your

Verse

B7

stock-ings　and check out ___ your fire - place. ___

E9

I think I got a log, ___ now.　that will fit　right in place.

B7　F#9

Give me ___ some of yours, ___

F9　E9

I'll give you ___ some of mine. ___　Yeah, it's Christ-mas time.

⊕ Coda

D.S. al Coda

B7

Outro

E9　B7　A B♭ B7

Yeah. ___

Additional Lyrics

2. Don't your ornaments look pretty
Hangin' on your Christmas tree?
I don't know 'bout no one else,
They sure look good to me.
Give me some of yours,
I'll give you some of mine,
'Cause it's Christmas time.

3. I got a big ol' candy cane
That you'd like to lick.
If you take your time,
Ooh, that'll do the trick.
Now give me some of yours,
I'll give you some of mine,
'Cause it's Christmas time.

Dig That Crazy Santa Claus

Words and Music by Albert Johnston Jr., Leon Rene and Rafael Rene

INTRO
Fast Shuffle ♩ = 188

VERSE

1. Dig that cra-zy San-ta Claus, with his red suit on.
2., D.S. See additional lyrics

To Coda 1

Dig that walk, that cra-zy talk. A man, oh, man, he's real-ly gone.

CHORUS

Cool it, Ru-dolph, cool it, a with your nose a-glow.

D.S. al Coda 1

Tell those groov-y rein-deer, when San-ta starts to blow. Go, go.

Coda 1

INTERLUDE

Christ-mas Eve. Jump.

Additional lyrics

2., 4. DIG THAT CRAZY SANTA CLAUS WITH HIS BAG OF TOYS.
DRAGS HIS SACK THROUGH A CHIMNEY STACK,
ALL THE LITTLE HEP-CATS JUMP FOR JOY.

D.S., D.S.S. DIG THAT CRAZY SANTA CLAUS, WELL I DO BELIEVE
HE WILL BRING SOME CRAZY TOYS.
YOU BETTER BE GOOD THIS CHRISTMAS EVE.

Merry Christmas, Baby

Words and Music by Lou Baxter
and Johnny Moore

Please Come Home for Christmas

Words and Music by Charles Brown
and Gene Redd

Santa Baby

By Joan Javits,
Phil Springer and Tony Springer

Additional lyrics

2. Santa baby, a '54 convertible too, light blue,
   I'll wait up for you, dear,
   Santa baby, so hurry down the chimney tonight.

4. Santa honey, one little thing I really need: the deed
   To a platinum mine.
   Santa baby, so hurry down the chimney tonight.

5. Santa cutie, and fill my stocking with a duplex and checks,
   Sign your X on the line.
   Santa cutie, and hurry down the chimney tonight.

6. Santa baby, forgot to mention one little thing, a ring.
   I don't mean on the phone.
   Santa baby, so hurry down the chimney tonight.

Soulful Christmas

Words and Music by Hank Ballard, James Brown and Alfred Ellis

Outro

Additional Lyrics

2. Got my baby, my precious love.
Happiness, good God, I got plenty of.
Would you believe I got peace of mind?
And I'll be groovin' at Christmas time.
Merry Christmas, Happy New Year.

3. Hope you have a good cheer.
I love you, James Brown love you.
Your luck is so and so, missin' you.
Brother love, ow, ow.

4. Soulful Christmas, like a sweet melody,
I'm a lucky so and so, the bells gonna ring for me.
Merry Christmas and a Happy New Year
To all of my fans, have good cheer.
I love you, I love you, won't take nobody else.
I can't stand myself, huh, good God.

5. I got a heart full of love for the whole wide world.
And a little special love, a little soulful girl.
I got this feelin' every, every now and then
Gotta get ready, bring the New Year in.
Merry Christmas and a Happy New Year.

Back Door Santa

Words and Music by Marcus Lewis Daniel and Clarence George Carter

BUT ONCE A YEAR. BUT I'LL COME RUN-NIN' WITH MY PRES-ENTS

EV-'RY TIME YOU CALL ME DEAR. I KEEP SOME

BRIDGE

CHANGE IN MY POCK-ET IN CASE THE CHIL-DREN WERE AT HOME. I GIVE THEM A FEW PEN-NIES SO

WE CAN BE A-LONE. I LEAVE THE BACK DOOR O-PEN SO IF AN-Y-BOD-Y SMELLS A MOUSE WOULD-N'T OL'

CHORUS

SAN-TA BE IN TROU-BLE IF IT AIN'T NO CHIM-NEY IN THE HOUSE. I'M A BACK DOOR SAN-TA.

MAKE MY RUNS A-BOUT THE BREAK O' DAY.

I MAKE THE WOM-EN HAP-PY WHILE THE MEN ARE OUT AT PLAY.

GUITAR SOLO

TO CODA

D.S. AL CODA

CODA

I KEEP SOME

Blue Christmas

Words and Music by Billy Hayes
and Jay Johnson

BLUE _____ MEM - 'RIES _____ START _____ CALL - IN'.

YOU'LL BE DO - IN' AL - RIGHT _____ WITH YOUR

CHRIST - MAS OF WHITE, BUT I'LL _____ HAVE A BLUE, _____

_____ BLUE, BLUE, BLUE CHRIST - MAS.

INTERLUDE

OUTRO

YOU'LL BE DO - IN' AL - RIGHT _____ WITH YOUR

CHRIST - MAS OF WHITE, _____ BUT I'LL HAVE A BLUE, _____

_____ BLUE, _____ BLUE, BLUE CHRIST - MAS. _____

𝄢 C Version

Christmas Time

Words and Music by Bruce Iglauer, Ed Williams and James Young

ADDITIONAL LYRICS

2. Don't your ornaments look pretty
   Hangin' on your Christmas tree?
   I don't know 'bout no one else.
   They sure look good to me.
   Give me some of yours.
   I'll give you some of mine,
   'Cause it's Christmas time.

3. I got a big ol' candy cane
   That you'd like to lick.
   If you take your time,
   Ooh, that'll do the trick.
   Now give me some of yours.
   I'll give you some of mine,
   'Cause it's Christmas time.

Additional lyrics

2., 4. Dig that crazy Santa Claus with his bag of toys.
Drags his sack through a chimney stack,
All the little hep-cats jump for joy.

D.S., D.S.S. Dig that crazy Santa Claus, well I do believe
He will bring some crazy toys.
You better be good this Christmas Eve.

Merry Christmas, Baby

Words and Music by Lou Baxter
and Johnny Moore

Please Come Home for Christmas

Words and Music by Charles Brown
and Gene Redd

Santa Baby

By Joan Javits,
Phil Springer and Tony Springer

© 1953 Trinity Music, Inc.
Copyright Renewed 1981 and Controlled in the U.S. by Philip Springer
Copyright Controlled for the world outside the U.S. by Alley Music Corp. and Bug Music-Trio Music Company
International Copyright Secured   All Rights Reserved

ADDITIONAL LYRICS

2. Santa baby, a '54 convertible too, light blue,
   I'll wait up for you, dear,
   Santa Baby, so hurry down the chimney tonight.

4. Santa honey, one little thing I really need: the deed
   To a platinum mine.
   Santa baby, so hurry down the chimney tonight.

5. Santa cutie, and fill my stocking with a duplex and checks,
   Sign your X on the line.
   Santa cutie, and hurry down the chimney tonight.

6. Santa baby, forgot to mention one little thing, a ring.
   I don't mean on the phone.
   Santa baby, so hurry down the chimney tonight.

Soulful Christmas

Words and Music by Hank Ballard,
James Brown and Alfred Ellis

Outro

YEAR.   ALL GOOD CHEER.   THERE'S ONE MORE THING,   YOU BEEN SO NICE

TO ME   DOWN ___ THROUGH THE YEARS. ___   AND I'LL AL-WAYS RE-

MEM-BER YOU. ___   WELL I'LL NEV-ER FOR-GET,   YOU BOUGHT MY REC-ORDS,   COME TO SEE MY SHOW.

THAT'S ___ WHY JAMES ___ BROWN ___   LOVE YOU ___

___ SO.   YOU COME TO SEE MY SHOW. ___   THAT'S A DEBT   THAT I'LL AL - WAYS

OWE. ___   COME TO SEE MY SHOW. ___   SEE YOU AT CHRIST-MAS,   COME TO SEE MY

SHOW.   SEE MY SHOW. ___

Additional Lyrics

2. GOT MY BABY, MY PRECIOUS LOVE,
HAPPINESS, GOOD GOD, I GOT PLENTY OF.
WOULD YOU BELIEVE I GOT PEACE OF MIND?
AND I'LL BE GROOVIN' AT CHRISTMAS TIME.
MERRY CHRISTMAS, HAPPY NEW YEAR.

3. HOPE YOU HAVE A GOOD CHEER.
I LOVE YOU, JAMES BROWN LOVE YOU.
YOUR LUCK IS SO AND SO, MISSIN' YOU.
BROTHER LOVE, OW, OW.

4. SOULFUL CHRISTMAS, LIKE A SWEET MELODY,
I'M A LUCKY SO AND SO, THE BELLS GONNA RING FOR ME.
MERRY CHRISTMAS AND A HAPPY NEW YEAR
TO ALL OF MY FANS, HAVE GOOD CHEER.
I LOVE YOU, I LOVE YOU, WON'T TAKE NOBODY ELSE.
I CAN'T STAND MYSELF, HUH, GOOD GOD.

5. I GOT A HEART FULL OF LOVE FOR THE WHOLE WIDE WORLD.
AND A LITTLE SPECIAL LOVE, A LITTLE SOULFUL GIRL.
I GOT THIS FEELIN' EVERY, EVERY NOW AND THEN
GOTTA GET READY, BRING THE NEW YEAR IN.
MERRY CHRISTMAS AND A HAPPY NEW YEAR.

HAL•LEONARD BLUES PLAY-ALONG

For use with all the C, B♭, Bass Clef and E♭ Instruments, the Hal Leonard Blues Play-Along Series is the ultimate jamming tool for all blues musicians.

With easy-to-read lead sheets, and other split-track choices on the included CD, these first-of-a-kind packages will bring your local blues jam right into your house! Each song on the CD includes two tracks: a full stereo mix, and a split track mix with removable guitar, bass, piano, and harp parts. The CD is playable on any CD player, and is also enhanced so Mac and PC users can adjust the recording to any tempo without changing the pitch!

1. Chicago Blues
All Your Love (I Miss Loving) • Easy Baby • I Ain't Got You • I'm Your Hoochie Coochie Man • Killing Floor • Mary Had a Little Lamb • Messin' with the Kid • Sweet Home Chicago.
00843106 Book/CD Pack $12.99

2. Texas Blues
Hide Away • If You Love Me Like You Say • Mojo Hand • Okie Dokie Stomp • Pride and Joy • Reconsider Baby • T-Bone Shuffle • The Things That I Used to Do.
00843107 Book/CD Pack $12.99

3. Slow Blues
Don't Throw Your Love on Me So Strong • Five Long Years • I Can't Quit You Baby • I Just Want to Make Love to You • The Sky Is Crying • (They Call It) Stormy Monday (Stormy Monday Blues) • Sweet Little Angel • Texas Flood.
00843108 Book/CD Pack $12.99

4. Shuffle Blues
Beautician Blues • Bright Lights, Big City • Further on up the Road • I'm Tore Down • Juke • Let Me Love You Baby • Look at Little Sister • Rock Me Baby.
00843171 Book/CD Pack $12.99

5. B.B. King
Everyday I Have the Blues • It's My Own Fault Darlin' • Just Like a Woman • Please Accept My Love • Sweet Sixteen • The Thrill Is Gone • Why I Sing the Blues • You Upset Me Baby.
00843172 Book/CD Pack $14.99

6. Jazz Blues
Birk's Works • Blues in the Closet • Cousin Mary • Freddie Freeloader • Now's the Time • Tenor Madness • Things Ain't What They Used to Be • Turnaround.
00843175 Book/CD Pack $12.99

7. Howlin' Wolf
Built for Comfort • Forty-Four • How Many More Years • Killing Floor • Moanin' at Midnight • Shake for Me • Sitting on Top of the World • Smokestack Lightning.
00843176 Book/CD Pack $12.99

8. Blues Classics
Baby, Please Don't Go • Boom Boom • Born Under a Bad Sign • Dust My Broom • How Long, How Long Blues • I Ain't Superstitious • It Hurts Me Too • My Babe.
00843177 Book/CD Pack $12.99

9. Albert Collins
Brick • Collins' Mix • Don't Lose Your Cool • Frost Bite • Frosty • I Ain't Drunk • Master Charge • Trash Talkin'.
00843178 Book/CD Pack $12.99

10. Uptempo Blues
Cross Road Blues (Crossroads) • Give Me Back My Wig • Got My Mo Jo Working • The House Is Rockin' • Paying the Cost to Be the Boss • Rollin' and Tumblin' • Turn on Your Love Light • You Can't Judge a Book by the Cover.
00843179 Book/CD Pack $12.99

11. Christmas Blues
Back Door Santa • Blue Christmas • Dig That Crazy Santa Claus • Merry Christmas, Baby • Please Come Home for Christmas • Santa Baby • Soulful Christmas.
00843203 Book/CD Pack $12.99

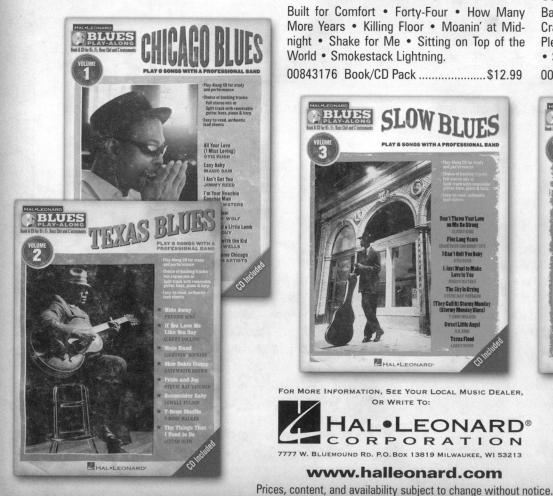

FOR MORE INFORMATION, SEE YOUR LOCAL MUSIC DEALER, OR WRITE TO:

HAL•LEONARD® CORPORATION
7777 W. BLUEMOUND RD. P.O. BOX 13819 MILWAUKEE, WI 53213

www.halleonard.com

Prices, content, and availability subject to change without notice.

0910

For use with all B-flat, E-flat, Bass Clef and C instruments, the Jazz Play-Along® Series is the ultimate learning tool for all jazz musicians. With musician-friendly lead sheets, melody cues, and other split-track choices on the included CD, these first-of-a-kind packages help you master improvisation while playing some of the greatest tunes of all time. FOR STUDY, each tune includes a split track with: melody cue with proper style and inflection • professional rhythm tracks • choruses for soloing • removable bass part • removable piano part. FOR PERFORMANCE, each tune also has: an additional full stereo accompaniment track (no melody) • additional choruses for soloing.

56. **"GEORGIA ON MY MIND" & OTHER SONGS BY HOAGY CARMICHAEL**
00843056 ......$15.99

57. **VINCE GUARALDI**
00843057 ......$16.99

58. **MORE LENNON AND MCCARTNEY**
00843059 ......$15.99

59. **SOUL JAZZ**
00843060 ......$15.99

60. **DEXTER GORDON**
00843061 ......$15.95

61. **MONGO SANTAMARIA**
00843062 ......$15.95

62. **JAZZ-ROCK FUSION**
00843063 ......$14.95

63. **CLASSICAL JAZZ**
00843064 ......$14.95

64. **TV TUNES**
00843065 ......$14.95

65. **SMOOTH JAZZ**
00843066 ......$16.99

66. **A CHARLIE BROWN CHRISTMAS**
00843067 ......$16.99

67. **CHICK COREA**
00843068 ......$15.95

68. **CHARLES MINGUS**
00843069 ......$16.95

69. **CLASSIC JAZZ**
00843071 ......$15.99

70. **THE DOORS**
00843072 ......$14.95

71. **COLE PORTER CLASSICS**
00843073 ......$14.95

72. **CLASSIC JAZZ BALLADS**
00843074 ......$15.99

73. **JAZZ/BLUES**
00843075 ......$14.95

74. **BEST JAZZ CLASSICS**
00843076 ......$15.99

75. **PAUL DESMOND**
00843077 ......$14.95

76. **BROADWAY JAZZ BALLADS**
00843078 ......$15.99

77. **JAZZ ON BROADWAY**
00843079 ......$15.99

78. **STEELY DAN**
00843070 ......$14.99

79. **MILES DAVIS CLASSICS**
00843081 ......$15.99

80. **JIMI HENDRIX**
00843083 ......$15.99

81. **FRANK SINATRA – CLASSICS**
00843084 ......$15.99

82. **FRANK SINATRA – STANDARDS**
00843085 ......$15.99

83. **ANDREW LLOYD WEBBER**
00843104 ......$14.95

84. **BOSSA NOVA CLASSICS**
00843105 ......$14.95

85. **MOTOWN HITS**
00843109 ......$14.95

86. **BENNY GOODMAN**
00843110 ......$14.95

87. **DIXIELAND**
00843111 ......$14.95

88. **DUKE ELLINGTON FAVORITES**
00843112 ......$14.95

89. **IRVING BERLIN FAVORITES**
00843113 ......$14.95

90. **THELONIOUS MONK CLASSICS**
00841262 ......$16.99

91. **THELONIOUS MONK FAVORITES**
00841263 ......$16.99

92. **LEONARD BERNSTEIN**
00450134 ......$15.99

93. **DISNEY FAVORITES**
00843142 ......$14.99

94. **RAY**
00843143 ......$14.99

95. **JAZZ AT THE LOUNGE**
00843144 ......$14.99

96. **LATIN JAZZ STANDARDS**
00843145 ......$14.99

97. **MAYBE I'M AMAZED**
00843148 ......$15.99

98. **DAVE FRISHBERG**
00843149 ......$15.99

99. **SWINGING STANDARDS**
00843150 ......$14.99

100. **LOUIS ARMSTRONG**
00740423 ......$15.99

101. **BUD POWELL**
00843152 ......$14.99

102. **JAZZ POP**
00843153 ......$14.99

103. **ON GREEN DOLPHIN STREET & OTHER JAZZ CLASSICS**
00843154 ......$14.99

104. **ELTON JOHN**
00843155 ......$14.99

105. **SOULFUL JAZZ**
00843151 ......$15.99

106. **SLO' JAZZ**
00843117 ......$14.99

107. **MOTOWN CLASSICS**
00843116 ......$14.99

108. **JAZZ WALTZ**
00843159 ......$15.99

109. **OSCAR PETERSON**
00843160 ......$15.99

110. **JUST STANDARDS**
00843161 ......$15.99

111. **COOL CHRISTMAS**
00843162 ......$15.99

114. **MODERN JAZZ QUARTET FAVORITES**
00843163 ......$15.99

115. **THE SOUND OF MUSIC**
00843164 ......$15.99

116. **JACO PASTORIUS**
00843165 ......$15.99

117. **ANTONIO CARLOS JOBIM – MORE HITS**
00843166 ......$15.99

118. **BIG JAZZ STANDARDS COLLECTION**
00843167 ......$27.50

119. **JELLY ROLL MORTON**
00843168 ......$15.99

120. **J.S. BACH**
00843169 ......$15.99

121. **DJANGO REINHARDT**
00843170 ......$15.99

122. **PAUL SIMON**
00843182 ......$16.99

123. **BACHARACH & DAVID**
00843185 ......$15.99

124. **JAZZ-ROCK HORN HITS**
00843186 ......$15.99

126. **COUNT BASIE CLASSICS**
00843157 ......$15.99

Jazz Instruction & Improvisation

Books for All Instruments from Hal Leonard

AN APPROACH TO JAZZ IMPROVISATION
by Dave Pozzi
Musicians Institute Press

 INCLUDES TAB

Explore the styles of Charlie Parker, Sonny Rollins, Bud Powell and others with this comprehensive guide to jazz improvisation. Covers: scale choices • chord analysis • phrasing • melodies • harmonic progressions • more.
00695135 Book/CD Pack $17.95

BUILDING A JAZZ VOCABULARY
By Mike Steinel

A valuable resource for learning the basics of jazz from Mike Steinel of the University of North Texas. It covers: the basics of jazz • how to build effective solos • a comprehensive practice routine • and a jazz vocabulary of the masters.
00849911 ....$19.95

THE CYCLE OF FIFTHS
by Emile and Laura De Cosmo

This essential instruction book provides more than 450 exercises, including hundreds of melodic and rhythmic ideas. The book is designed to help improvisors master the cycle of fifths, one of the primary progressions in music. Guaranteed to refine technique, enhance improvisational fluency, and improve sight-reading!
00311114 ....$16.99

THE DIATONIC CYCLE
by Emile and Laura De Cosmo

Renowned jazz educators Emile and Laura De Cosmo provide more than 300 exercises to help improvisors tackle one of music's most common progressions: the diatonic cycle. This book is guaranteed to refine technique, enhance improvisational fluency, and improve sight-reading!
00311115 ....$16.95

EAR TRAINING
by Keith Wyatt, Carl Schroeder and Joe Elliott
Musicians Institute Press

Covers: basic pitch matching • singing major and minor scales • identifying intervals • transcribing melodies and rhythm • identifying chords and progressions • seventh chords and the blues • modal interchange, chromaticism, modulation • and more.
00695198 Book/2-CD Pack...................$24.95

EXERCISES AND ETUDES FOR THE JAZZ INSTRUMENTALIST
by J.J. Johnson

Designed as study material and playable by any instrument, these pieces run the gamut of the jazz experience, featuring common and uncommon time signatures and keys, and styles from ballads to funk. They are progressively graded so that both beginners and professionals will be challenged by the demands of this wonderful music.
00842018 Bass Clef Edition....................$16.95
00842042 Treble Clef Edition..................$16.95

JAZZOLOGY
THE ENCYCLOPEDIA OF JAZZ THEORY FOR ALL MUSICIANS
by Robert Rawlins and Nor Eddine Bahha

This comprehensive resource covers a variety of jazz topics, for beginners and pros of any instrument. The book serves as an encyclopedia for reference, a thorough methodology for the student, and a workbook for the classroom.
00311167 ....$18.95

JAZZ JAM SESSION
15 TRACKS INCLUDING RHYTHM CHANGES, BLUES, BOSSA, BALLADS & MORE
by Ed Friedland

Bring your local jazz jam session home! These essential jazz rhythm grooves feature a professional rhythm section and are perfect for guitar, harmonica, keyboard, saxophone and trumpet players to hone their soloing skills. The feels, tempos and keys have been varied to broaden your jazz experience. Styles include: ballads, bebop, blues, bossa nova, cool jazz, and more, with improv guidelines for each track.
_____ 00311827 Book/CD Pack $19.99

JAZZ THEORY RESOURCES
by Bert Ligon
Houston Publishing, Inc.

This is a jazz theory text in two volumes. **Volume 1 includes:** review of basic theory • rhythm in jazz performance • triadic generalization • diatonic harmonic progressions and analysis • substitutions and turnarounds • and more. **Volume 2 includes:** modes and modal frameworks • quartal harmony • extended tertian structures and triadic superimposition • pentatonic applications • coloring "outside" the lines and beyond • and more.
00030458 Volume 1 ....$39.95
00030459 Volume 2 ....$29.95

JOY OF IMPROV
by Dave Frank and John Amaral

This book/CD course on improvisation for all instruments and all styles will help players develop monster musical skills! **Book One** imparts a solid basis in technique, rhythm, chord theory, ear training and improv concepts. **Book Two** explores more advanced chord voicings, chord arranging techniques and more challenging blues and melodic lines. The CD can be used as a listening and play-along tool.
00220005 Book 1 – Book/CD Pack $27.99
00220006 Book 2 – Book/CD Pack $24.95

THE PATH TO JAZZ IMPROVISATION
by Emile and Laura De Cosmo

This fascinating jazz instruction book offers an innovative, scholarly approach to the art of improvisation. It includes in-depth analysis and lessons about: cycle of fifths • diatonic cycle • overtone series • pentatonic scale • harmonic and melodic minor scale • polytonal order of keys • blues and bebop scales • modes • and more.
00310904 ....$14.95

THE SOURCE
THE DICTIONARY OF CONTEMPORARY AND TRADITIONAL SCALES
by Steve Barta

This book serves as an informative guide for people who are looking for good, solid information regarding scales, chords, and how they work together. It provides right and left hand fingerings for scales, chords, and complete inversions. Includes over 20 different scales, each written in all 12 keys.
00240885 ....$15.95

21 BEBOP EXERCISES
by Steve Rawlins

This book/CD pack is both a warm-up collection and a manual for bebop phrasing. Its tasty and sophisticated exercises will help you develop your proficiency with jazz interpretation. It concentrates on practice in all twelve keys – moving higher by half-step – to help develop dexterity and range. The companion CD includes all of the exercises in 12 keys.
00315341 Book/CD Pack $17.95

FOR MORE INFORMATION, SEE YOUR LOCAL MUSIC DEALER, OR WRITE TO:

HAL•LEONARD® CORPORATION
7777 W. BLUEMOUND RD. P.O. BOX 13819 MILWAUKEE, WI 53213

Prices, contents & availability subject to change without notice.

Visit Hal Leonard online at
www.halleonard.com

0910